# A New True Book

# CANCER

## By Dennis B. Fradin

Consultant: Gerald Gilchrist, M.D.
Chairman, Department of Radiation
MAYO Clinic, Rochester, Minnesota

CHILDRENS PRESS ®

CHICAGO

Smoking is one cause of lung cancer.

PHOTO CREDITS

Root Resources:
© MacDonald Photography—2, 19 (right), 36, 44 (left)
© Gail Nachel—14
© Grete Schoidt—31
© John Kohout—33 (bottom)
© Mary A. Root—40
© Jack Monsarratt—43 (right)

Cameramann International—Cover, 4, 7 (right), 11, 19, 21, 22, 27 (2 photos), 29, 33 (top), 35, 38

Journalism Services:
© Scott Wanner—7 (left), 18, 19 (left)
© 1986 by SIU—8, 12
© Paul F. Gero—17 (left)
© Steve Sumner—43 (left)
© Paul E. Burd—44 (right)
© Richard Derr—45

Custom Medical Stock Photo—17 (right)

Nawrocki Stock Photo:
© T. J. Florian—32

Courtesy: American Cancer Society—24

Cover: Patient receives radiation treatment.

Library of Congress Cataloging-in-Publication Data

Fradin, Dennis B.
   Cancer / by Dennis B. Fradin.
      p.    cm. — (A New true book)
   Includes index.
   Summary: Examines the various forms of cancer, their possible causes, and treatments, and discusses who can get cancer and what is being done to prevent or cure it.
   ISBN 0-516-01210-X
   1. Cancer—Juvenile literature. [1. Cancer.] I. Title.
RC263.F68  1988                    87-33790
616.99′4—dc19                      CIP
                                   AC

Childrens Press®, Chicago
Copyright ©1988 by Regensteiner Publishing Enterprises, Inc.
All rights reserved. Published simultaneously in Canada.
Printed in the United States of America.
1 2 3 4 5 6 7 8 9 10 R 97 96 95 94 93 92 91 90 89 88

# TABLE OF CONTENTS

Each year cancer kills millions of people.

# WHAT IS CANCER?

The disease cancer is one of the leading killers of people.

You must know a bit about the human body to understand cancer. The body is made of many billions of tiny units called *cells*. Each day, millions of cells die. In healthy people, enough new cells are produced each minute to replace the ones that die.

Sometimes, though, a person's body produces too many new cells in a certain part of the body. This can build up a mass of extra tissue called a tumor. In some tumors, the cells are not too different from normal cells. Such tumors reach a certain point and then stop growing. They do not spread

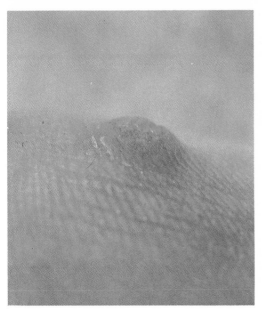

Most warts (left) or "beauty spots" (right) are not dangerous. However, if they grow or change in appearance they should be checked by a doctor.

through the body. These tumors are called *benign* (meaning "good") tumors. A person with a benign tumor does not have cancer. Warts or "beauty spots" are actually benign tumors.

In other tumors, the cells
are much different from
normal cells and grow out
of control. Such tumors
can badly damage the

This tumor grew on the spinal cord.

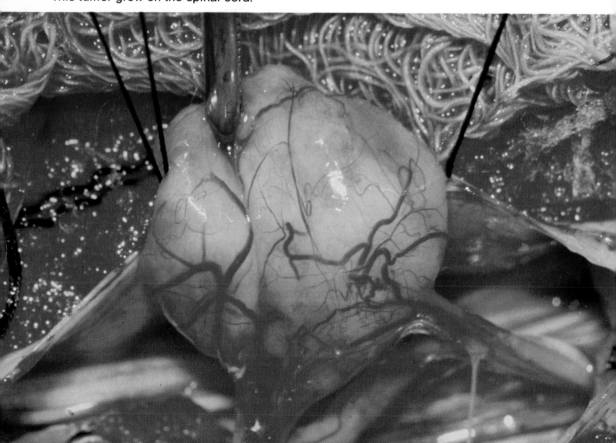

organs where they are growing. They can spread to other parts of the body, and kill the victim. These tumors are called *malignant* (meaning "evil") tumors. A person with a malignant tumor has cancer.

# WHO GETS CANCER?

People of any age can get cancer. Babies have had cancer. Babies have even been born with the disease. At the other end of the age scale, people have developed cancer at 100 years of age and older.

Cancer is rare among children, though. It is more common among middle-aged people. And it is very common among the elderly.

# WHERE DOES CANCER STRIKE?

Exercise is important.

Cancer can strike any part of the body except the hair and nails. But there are places where it is especially common. The breathing organs called lungs are prone to cancer. The large intestine and other organs that help digest food are subject to the disease. Other organs where cancer strikes

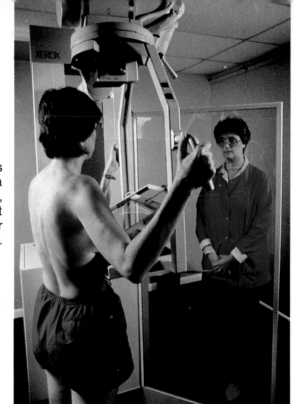

This woman is having a mammography, an X ray that checks for breast tumors.

include the skin, the bladder, the kidneys, the brain, the female breasts, and the male prostate gland. Cancer can even affect the blood. A common cancer in which abnormal white blood cells

are produced is called
leukemia.

One of the biggest
dangers of cancer is that
it can spread from one
organ to another. The
spread of cancer from the
first site to other places is
called *metastasis*. If the
cancer spreads to the liver
or another vital organ, the
patient will probably die.

Even the word cancer
reminds us of the
disease's tendency to
spread. Cancer comes

Ghost crab

from Latin and Greek
words meaning crab. A
crab's legs and claws
spread out in all directions
from its body. In the same
way, cancer can spread
through the body from the
original site.

# WHAT CAUSES CANCER?

Some people worry that they will "catch" cancer from cancer patients. Cancer is not catching. Every day, thousands of doctors and nurses work with cancer patients without catching the disease.

For the most part cancer seems to be caused by certain things in our environment, or surroundings.

In recent years, doctors have learned some of those causes. Substances that cause cancer are called *carcinogens*. Not everyone exposed to carcinogens develops cancer. Other factors in people's bodies seem to allow carcinogens to produce cancer in certain people.

Cigarettes contain many carcinogens. Smoking causes more than four out of every five cases of lung cancer. Smoking has also

Smoking causes more than four out of every five cases of lung cancer.

been linked to cancers of the mouth, bladder, and several other organs. In fact, cigarettes are involved in about three of every ten cancer deaths.

Certain chemicals and minerals also contain

carcinogens. For example, exposure to some dyes and oil products over long periods can cause cancer. So can breathing in small pieces of a mineral called asbestos.

Radiation (energy that moves in the form of waves or particles) can cause cancer, too. Most

Asbestos, used to insulate pipes and other objects, can cause cancer.

Too much exposure to radiation and the rays of the sun may cause some types of cancer.

skin cancers result from too much exposure to the sun's rays. Nuclear radiation from bombs and power plants can bring on the disease, as can too much exposure to X rays.

Knowing the causes of

cancer helps us avoid the disease. Simply by not smoking, we can greatly reduce our chances of getting lung cancer. We can further reduce our cancer risk by avoiding excessive radiation and chemicals that have been linked to the disease.

The causes of many cancers are not yet known. For example, the causes of leukemia and cancers of the digestive organs are still a mystery.

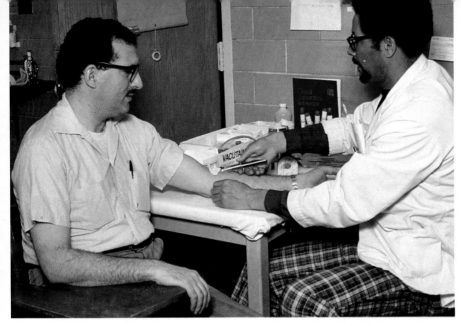

Some types of cancer show up on blood tests.

# CAN CANCER PATIENTS GET WELL?

Some people think that cancer is a death sentence. They hear that a person has cancer and assume that he or she will die. More than half of all

Blood samples are checked in a laboratory.

cancer victims (not counting skin cancer cases) do die of the disease. But cancer is NOT a death sentence. Millions of people who once had cancer are now living normal, healthy lives.

Here are the facts, as of 1987. Not counting skin cancer cases, of every ten Americans who get cancer, about six will die of it within five years. The other four will get well. Doctors don't say they are "cured," because they can't guarantee that the cancer won't ever come back.

Doctors who treat cancer patients are called *oncologists*. Oncologists have several ways to help cancer patients.

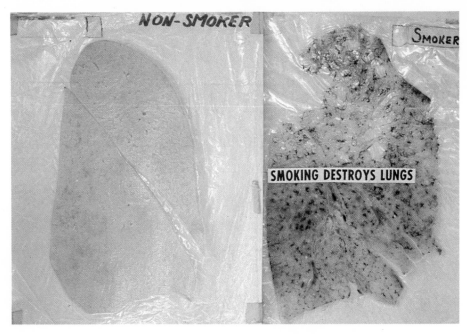

Healthy lung (left) and a diseased lung (right)
clearly show what happens to the lungs of smokers.

The main way doctors
conquer cancer is by
cutting out the tumor
through surgery. If a doctor
can operate before the
cancer has spread, there
is a good chance that all

traces of the disease can be wiped out. The key is finding the cancer early, *before* it has spread. Once cancer has metastasized to other organs, treatment becomes more complicated and difficult. When the cancer spreads, doctors are often helpless against the disease. Many people who have died of cancer would be alive today if they had sought medical help a little earlier.

Doctors also fight cancer

with certain drugs. The use of drugs to combat cancer is called *chemotherapy*. In recent years, chemotherapy has been used successfully against leukemia and other cancers. In fact, drugs have destroyed all traces of leukemia in the bodies of many patients.

Although radiation can cause cancer, it can also be very effective in shrinking and even curing

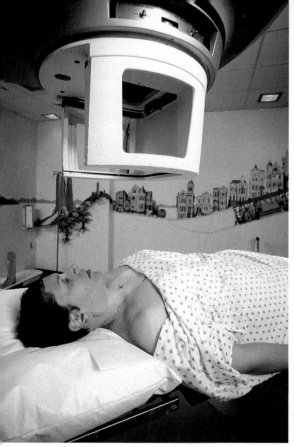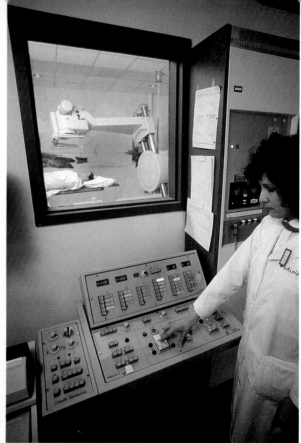

Patient (left) receives radiation therapy. A computer (right) controls the amount of radiation a patient receives.

tumors. X rays and gamma rays are two kinds of radiation that are aimed at certain cancers. However, not all cancers are sensitive to the effect of radiation.

Doctors sometimes use several methods to fight cancer. They call this combination therapy. They may shrink a tumor with X rays, then operate on it, and then use chemotherapy to destroy the last remaining cancer cells. Successful treatment seems to depend on getting rid of the last cancer cell.

Tissue samples, mounted on glass slides, are examined under a microscope.

# CANCER RESEARCH

Thousands of scientists in hospitals and research centers around the world are working to conquer cancer. These scientists are known as cancer researchers. Some cancer researchers experiment on mice and other animals to learn more about the disease.

Many researchers are trying to learn more about the causes of cancer. For example, scientists suspect that certain foods cause certain digestive system

Fried foods and meats high in fat, such as bacon and sausage, should be limited in a healthy diet.

Fresh fruits and vegetables are an important part of a healthy diet.

cancers. Researchers give these foods to mice to see if they produce cancer. They also interview human patients to determine what foods may have caused them to get cancer.

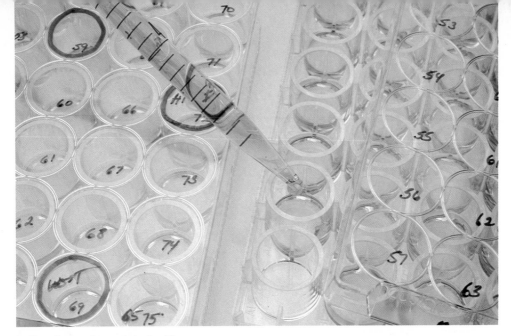

Cell cultures, inoculated with
a virus, are used in cancer studies.

How much radiation
does it take to cause
cancer? How great a
cancer hazard is pollution?
Are viruses involved in
some cancers? These
questions are also being
studied by those who want

Scientists study the relationship between air pollution and some forms of cancer.

to learn more about the causes of cancer.

Other researchers are creating better ways for doctors to *diagnose* cancer (determine that someone has the disease). This is important, because the sooner the cancer is diagnosed, the greater the chance to save the patient. Scientists are now working on blood tests and other new methods to

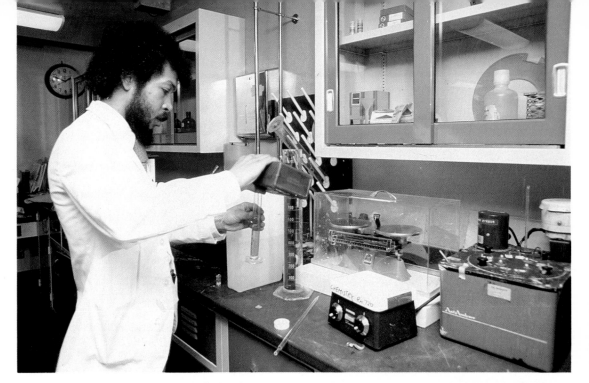

Scientists are looking for new blood tests that will accurately detect some cancers in their early stage of development.

detect very early cancers. These tests could save millions of lives in the 21st century.

Still other researchers are developing better cancer treatments. There

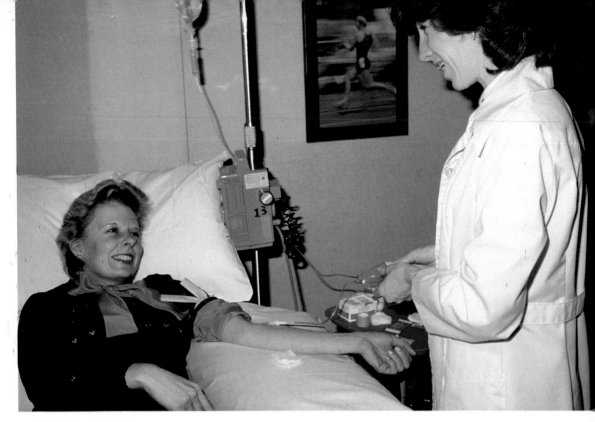

This patient is fighting her cancer with chemicals.

are about a hundred
different kinds of cancer.
Chemicals are constantly
being tested to see if they
work against various kinds
of cancer in animals and

people. Hundreds of thousands of chemicals have been tested thus far. Now and then scientists find one that works, and they add it to the list of the several dozen known cancer-fighting drugs.

How does cancer begin in the body? Why is cancer more common in certain families? Why does one person get cancer while another who lives the same kind of life remains healthy? Could a

Cancer research is taking place in laboratories all over the world

vaccine be developed to protect us from cancer? The conquest of cancer lies in the answers to these and other questions being addressed by cancer researchers.

# PROTECTING YOURSELF FROM CANCER

There are some ways
you can protect yourself
from cancer right now. For
one thing, promise yourself
that you won't smoke.
Smoking causes a great
number of cancer cases.
And smoking is also bad
for the heart and other organs.
If you make a vow to

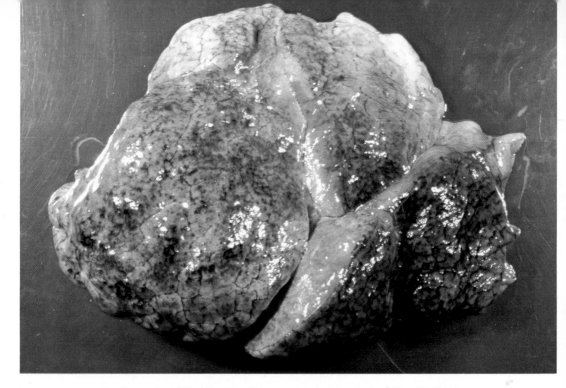

Lung cancer destroys healthy tissue, the surgeon general of the United States warns people about the dangers of smoking. It "causes lung cancer, heart disease, emphysema, and may complicate pregnancy."

never smoke, and if you keep your promise, you could be saving your own life.

Eat a well-balanced diet and don't eat too many fatty foods. Avoid excessive sunlight and wear protective clothing when out in the sun. Do not expose yourself to any chemicals, pollution, or radiation you can avoid.

See your doctor regularly. He or she can advise you further as to the best ways to avoid cancer and other diseases. And although most people will never get cancer, those who do get it have a good chance of surviving if they see their doctors early enough.

# HOPE FOR THE FUTURE

There is some good
news and some bad news
regarding cancer. The
good news is that a
greater percentage of
people are getting well
from cancer than ever
before. The bad news is
that more people than
ever before are getting
cancer. The American
Cancer Society says that a

child born in the United States in 1987 has more than a one in three chance of one day developing cancer.

The great hope for the future is that researchers

will find ways to keep this prediction from coming true. Perhaps they will find ways to prevent cancer. Perhaps they will even develop a drug that can wipe out the disease.

Other diseases have been conquered. For

Hopefully, advances in the detection and treatment of cancer will protect these youngsters.

example, smallpox has been wiped out. Hopefully cancer will one day be a disease of the past, too. You might even become a cancer researcher and help in the conquest of this terrible disease.

# WORDS YOU SHOULD KNOW

**asbestos**(az • BESS • tuss) — a mineral that can cause cancer

**benign tumor**(bih • NINE) — a tumor that is not cancerous

**billion** — one thousand million, 1,000,000,000

**cancer**(KAN • ser) — a disease in which cells divide too often

**cancer researchers**(KAN • ser REE • ser • cherz) — scientists who work to learn more about cancer

**carcinogens**(KAR • sin • eh • jenz) — substances that cause cancer

**cells**(SELS) — the tiny units of which animals and plants are made

**chemotherapy**(kee • moh • THAIR • ih • pee) — the use of drugs to combat cancer or other diseases

**combination therapy**(kahm • bih • NAY • shun THAIR • ih • pee) — the use of several treatment methods to help a cancer patient

**diagnose**(DYE • ig • nohss) — to determine what is wrong with a patient

**females**(FEE • mailz) — girls and women

**gamma rays**(GAM • ah RAIZ) — powerful radiation waves that are similar to X rays

**leukemia**(loo • KEE • mee • ya) — a cancer in which too many white blood cells are produced

**lungs**(LUNGZ) — the two main breathing organs in people and other mammals

**males**(MAILZ) — boys and men

**malignant tumor**(muh • LIG • nent TOO • mer) — a tumor that is cancerous

**metastasis**(meta • STAH • sis) — the spread of cancer from the first site to other places

**million**(mill • YUN) — a thousand thousand (1,000,000)

**nuclear radiation**(NOO • clee • er ray • dee • A • shun) — materials given off by atoms that are harmful in large quantities

**oncologists**(on • CAHL • oh • jists) — doctors who are cancer specialists

**pollution**(puh • LOO • shun) — the dirtying of our environment

**radiation**(ray • dee • A • shun) — energy that moves in the form of waves or particles

**tumor**(TOO • mer) — an abnormal growth of extra tissue

**viruses**(VYE • russ • iz) — very small organisms which can cause disease

**X rays**(X RAIZ) — a kind of radiation doctors use to see inside the body; X rays can be used to treat cancer, but in large amounts they can also cause cancer

# INDEX

## About the Author

*Dennis Fradin attended Northwestern University on a partial creative scholarship and was graduated in 1967. His previous books include the Young People's Stories of Our States series for Childrens Press, and Bad Luck Tony for Prentice—Hall. In the True book series Dennis has written about astronomy, farming, comets, archaeology, movies, space colonies, the space lab, explorers, and pioneers. He is married and the father of three children.*